AF485782

SONY A7R V

USER GUIDE

Manual for Mastering Dials, Buttons, Settings, Modes for Best Experience

By

Alan B. Haight

Copyright

This book is protected under copyright law. No part of this publication may be reproduced, distributed, or transmitted in any form or by any means, including photocopying, recording, or other electronic or mechanical methods, without the prior written permission of the publisher, except for brief quotations used in reviews and certain other noncommercial uses permitted by copyright law.

Dedication

To the photographers and videographers who see the world through a lens, capturing moments that would otherwise fade and revealing beauty that often goes unnoticed.

This book is dedicated to your passion, creativity, and relentless pursuit of excellence. May each page inspire you to push the boundaries of what's possible with the Sony A7R V and help you craft images that tell your unique story.

For those who never stop learning and those who never stop creating, this guide is for you.

Table of Contents

Chapter One

Introduction to the Sony A7R V

What's New in the Sony A7R V

The Sony A7R V is a powerful camera that packs advanced technology into a compact, mirrorless body. If you're familiar with Sony's A7 series, you'll notice some impressive upgrades here. Sony has added a new, improved autofocus system that can recognize and track subjects like people, animals, and even cars with incredible accuracy. The A7R V also includes a higher-resolution sensor for extremely detailed photos and supports 8K video recording.

This camera is designed for those who want sharp, high-quality images and smooth video. Sony has also made it easier to use with improved menus and customization options, making this model perfect for both beginners and experienced photographers.

Overview of Camera Specifications

Let's look at some of the main specifications:

- **Resolution**: 61 megapixels, meaning it captures a lot of detail.
- **Autofocus**: AI-based, which means it can track moving objects accurately.
- **Image Stabilization**: Built-in stabilization to keep your shots steady.
- **Video Quality**: Can record up to 8K video, offering extremely high-definition video recording.

- **Screen**: Tiltable LCD screen for easy shooting at different angles.
- **Battery Life**: Improved battery life compared to previous models, so you can shoot longer.

These specs make the A7R V an excellent choice for photographers looking to capture landscapes, portraits, and videos with sharpness and clarity.

Who Is This Camera For?

The Sony A7R V is ideal for:

- **Professional Photographers**: Those who need high-quality images and control over settings.
- **Videographers**: People who want top-notch video quality, including 8K resolution.
- **Hobbyists and Enthusiasts**: If you're serious about photography and want a camera that can grow with you, this is a great option.

This camera can handle almost any type of photography—from landscapes to portraits, sports to wildlife—making it versatile for a range of users.

Unboxing and Initial Setup

Let's unbox and set up your Sony A7R V!

1. **Open the Box Carefully**: Inside, you'll find the camera body, a battery, a battery charger, a USB cable, and a shoulder strap. There may also be a user manual, which is helpful for understanding more advanced features.
2. **Insert the Battery**: Open the battery compartment, located on the bottom of the camera. Insert the

battery, making sure it clicks in place. Close the compartment.

3. **Attach a Lens** (if you have one): Line up the white dot on the lens with the white dot on the camera body. Gently twist the lens until you hear a click, which means it's locked in place. You're ready to shoot!

4. **Power On the Camera**: Slide the power switch to "On." The camera should start up, and you'll see a display on the screen or viewfinder.

5. **Select Your Language and Time Zone**: The first time you turn it on, the camera will prompt you to set up your language, date, and time. This helps keep your files organized.

6. **Format the Memory Card** (if inserted): Insert the memory card into the slot. Navigate to the menu, find "Format," and select your card. This erases any previous data and gets the card ready for new photos.

Use Leading Lines

Natural or man-made lines, such as roads, rivers, fences, or pathways, can draw the viewer's eye directly to the subject. Leading lines not only create a sense of depth but also guide the viewer through the story you're trying to tell.

Chapter Two

Camera Body and Layout

Front, Back, and Side Views: Understanding the Physical Layout

The Sony A7R V is designed to be easy to hold and operate. It's packed with buttons and dials, each serving a unique purpose.

1. **Front of the Camera**:
   - **Lens Mount**: The large circular area on the front is where you attach your lens. The white dot on the mount is a guide to help you align the lens correctly.
   - **Lens Release Button**: Right next to the lens mount is a small button. Press this to detach the lens from the camera body.
   - **AF-Assist Lamp**: This little light near the lens mount helps with focusing in low-light conditions.
   - **Grip**: The textured grip on the right side helps you hold the camera securely, especially when shooting for extended periods.
2. **Back of the Camera**:
   - **LCD Screen**: The large screen is where you can review your photos, navigate menus, and even take photos using live view.
   - **Viewfinder**: Located above the screen, the viewfinder lets you frame your shots. It also displays essential settings when you look through it.
   - **Menu Button**: This button opens the camera's menu, giving you access to all settings and options.

- o **Playback Button**: The "Playback" button allows you to view photos and videos you've taken. Press it to review your shots.
- o **Delete Button**: When reviewing a photo or video, press this button to delete it if needed.
- o **AF-ON Button**: This button activates autofocus. It's useful for setting focus independently of the shutter button, allowing more control over your shots.
- o **Multi-Selector (Joystick)**: This little joystick helps you move through settings quickly or adjust your focus point. It's especially handy when you want to be precise with your focus.

3. **Top of the Camera**:
- o **Mode Dial**: This dial, usually on the left or right, allows you to switch between shooting modes like Auto, Manual, Aperture Priority, and more. It's one of the most important controls on the camera.
- o **Shutter Button**: Located near the grip, this is the button you press to take a picture. Press halfway down to focus, and fully press to capture the shot.
- o **Control Dials**: These dials adjust settings like shutter speed, aperture, and ISO. They're located near the shutter button and can be easily adjusted with your index finger and thumb.
- o **Hot Shoe**: This metal slot on top is for attaching external accessories like flashes or microphones.

4. **Side of the Camera**:
- o **Ports**: The A7R V has several ports on its side, including:
    - ▪ **HDMI Port**: For connecting the camera to an external monitor or TV.

- USB-C Port: Used for charging, transferring files, or connecting to a computer for tethered shooting.
    - **Microphone and Headphone Jacks**: These allow you to connect an external microphone for better audio and headphones for monitoring audio while recording video.
  - **Memory Card Slot**: On the side of the camera, there's a compartment for memory cards. This is where you store your photos and videos.

Buttons and Dials Overview

- **Mode Dial**: This is the big dial on top. It allows you to switch between different shooting modes, such as:
  - **Auto Mode**: The camera decides the settings for you, great for beginners.
  - **Aperture Priority (A)**: You set the aperture, and the camera adjusts the shutter speed.
  - **Shutter Priority (S)**: You control the shutter speed, and the camera handles the aperture.
  - **Manual (M)**: You have full control over both shutter speed and aperture.
- **Shutter Button**: Found on top, this button is used to take pictures. Press it halfway to focus, then press all the way to take a photo.
- **Control Dials**: There are front and back control dials. They let you adjust important settings:
  - **Shutter Speed**: Controls how long the camera sensor is exposed to light. Faster speeds freeze motion, while slower speeds create blur.
  - **Aperture**: Controls how much light enters through the lens. A lower aperture (e.g., $f/2.8$) creates a blurry background, while a higher

aperture (e.g., f/16) keeps more of the scene
in focus.

- o **ISO**: Controls the camera's sensitivity to light.
  A higher ISO brightens images but can add
  grain.
- **Custom Buttons** (C1, C2, etc.): These buttons can
  be customized to perform specific functions, like
  switching focus modes or adjusting ISO quickly. You
  can set these up in the camera menu to suit your
  workflow.

Memory Card Slots and Battery Compartment

1. **Memory Card Slots**:
   - o The Sony A7R V has dual memory card slots,
     meaning you can insert two memory cards at
     once. This is useful if you want to keep a
     backup of all your photos or use one card for
     photos and another for videos.
   - o To insert a memory card, open the side
     compartment, align the card with the slot, and
     push it in until it clicks. To remove it, gently
     press the card again to release it.
2. **Battery Compartment**:
   - o Located on the bottom of the camera, this
     compartment houses the battery.
   - o Open the compartment cover, insert the
     battery with the arrow facing in, and close the
     cover securely. The battery should fit snugly.
   - o To charge, use the USB-C port on the side or
     remove the battery and charge it with an
     external charger.

*Connecting External Devices: HDMI, USB-C, and
Audio Ports*

The Sony A7R V has a range of ports to connect other
devices, making it versatile for both photography and
videography.

1. **HDMI Port**:
    - Use the HDMI port to connect your camera
      to an external monitor or TV. This is
      particularly helpful for video recording, as you
      can see a larger preview of what you're
      filming.
2. **USB-C Port**:
    - This port serves multiple purposes. You can
      use it to transfer photos and videos to a
      computer, charge the battery, or shoot while
      connected to a computer (called tethered
      shooting).
3. **Microphone and Headphone Jacks**:
    - The microphone jack allows you to attach an
      external mic, which is great for capturing
      high-quality audio.
    - The headphone jack lets you monitor audio
      levels while recording video, ensuring the
      sound is clear.

Reflections in water, glass, or even puddles after rain can transform an ordinary scene into something extraordinary. Experiment with symmetry and composition to create stunning visual effects, adding a layer of intrigue to your shots.

Chapter Three

Exploring the Menu System

The Sony A7R V has a detailed menu system that lets you control almost every aspect of the camera. While it may seem complex at first, once you know where to find key settings, navigating it becomes much easier.

Introduction to the Sony A7R V Menu

The menu on the Sony A7R V is organized into different sections, each with specific functions. Here's a simple breakdown of the main menu tabs:

1. **Shooting Settings**: Adjusts camera settings for taking photos and videos.
2. **Exposure and Color**: Manages settings like ISO, white balance, and color profiles.
3. **Focus**: Controls autofocus settings and customization.
4. **Playback**: Manages how images and videos are displayed for review.
5. **Network**: Handles Wi-Fi, Bluetooth, and other connectivity options.
6. **Setup**: General settings for display, battery, memory card formatting, and more.

Each tab has its own list of sub-options, and we'll cover the most useful ones here.

How to Navigate the Menu

1. **Press the Menu Button**: Located on the back of the camera, this button opens the main menu.

2. **Use the Multi-Selector (Joystick)**: You can move up, down, left, or right to browse through the menu tabs and options.
3. **Select and Confirm Settings**: Once you highlight an option, press the center button on the joystick or the control wheel to enter a submenu or confirm your selection.
4. **Back Button**: To go back one step in the menu, press the "Menu" button again or use the "Back" option on the screen.

Key Settings to Customize

Let's look at some essential settings you may want to adjust right away. These settings can be customized based on your photography style or personal preferences.

1. **File Format** (in the Shooting Settings menu):
   - Choose between **JPEG** (smaller file size, easier to share) and **RAW** (larger file size, retains more details for editing). If you're new to photography, starting with JPEG is fine. If you plan to edit, RAW gives you more flexibility.
2. **Image Quality**:
   - **Extra Fine, Fine, Standard**: These options determine the level of compression for JPEG images. "Extra Fine" provides the highest quality.
3. **Focus Mode** (in the Focus menu):
   - Choose between **Single AF** (focuses once for still subjects), **Continuous AF** (tracks moving subjects), and **Manual Focus** (you adjust focus yourself). Continuous AF is ideal for action shots, while Single AF is best for stills.
4. **ISO Settings** (in Exposure and Color):

- o You can set **ISO Auto** if you want the camera to adjust the sensitivity to light automatically. This is great for quickly adapting to changes in lighting. For more control, you can set a specific ISO value manually.

5. **White Balance** (in Exposure and Color):
   - o Adjust the white balance to match the lighting in your environment. Options like **Daylight, Shade, Cloudy, Tungsten,** and **Fluorescent** help achieve accurate colors. If you're unsure, "Auto" works well in most cases.

6. **Metering Mode** (in Exposure and Color):
   - o **Multi, Center-Weighted,** and **Spot** are common options. Multi measures light across the whole scene, Center-Weighted focuses on the center area, and Spot measures a small specific area. Choose the one that best suits your subject.

7. **Focus Area** (in the Focus menu):
   - o Options include **Wide** (for capturing the entire scene), **Zone** (for focusing on specific areas), and **Flexible Spot** (for pinpoint accuracy on a small spot). Flexible Spot is ideal for portraits, while Wide works well for landscapes.

Using the My Menu Feature for Quick Access

The "My Menu" feature allows you to create a personalized menu for quick access to your favorite settings.

1. **Go to My Menu**: Open the menu and scroll to the "My Menu" tab.
2. **Add Your Favorite Settings**: Choose "Add Item" to select settings you use often, such as ISO, Focus Mode, or White Balance. This way, you don't have to scroll through the entire menu to find them.

3. **Organize Your My Menu**: Once added, you can rearrange the items in your preferred order. This allows you to quickly access important settings while shooting.

Tips for Efficient Menu Navigation

- **Customize Function Buttons**: Assign commonly used settings to the custom buttons (C1, C2, etc.) on the camera. This saves time by letting you adjust settings without opening the menu.
- **Use Touchscreen Navigation**: The A7R V has a touchscreen, which allows you to tap through some menu options. This can be faster than using the joystick.
- **Learn the Shortcuts**: As you use the camera more, you'll start to remember where your favorite settings are located. Practice makes it easier and faster over time.

Chapter Four

Buttons, Dials, and Their Functions

The Sony A7R V has several buttons and dials that let you control the camera settings quickly. Here, we'll explore each one, explaining how and when to use them. Let's go through them step by step.

The Mode Dial: Shooting Modes Explained

The Mode Dial is located on the top of the camera. It's one of the most important controls, as it lets you switch between different shooting modes. Here's what each mode does:

1. **Auto Mode** (green icon):
   - In Auto Mode, the camera chooses all the settings for you. This is perfect for beginners or quick snapshots when you don't have time to adjust settings manually.
2. **Aperture Priority Mode (A):**
   - In this mode, you set the aperture (the opening in the lens), which controls how much light enters the camera and affects depth of field. A lower aperture (e.g., f/2.8) creates a blurred background, while a higher aperture (e.g., f/16) keeps more of the scene in focus. The camera will automatically adjust the shutter speed to balance the exposure.
3. **Shutter Priority Mode (S):**
   - Here, you control the shutter speed, which determines how long the sensor is exposed to light. Faster speeds (e.g., 1/1000s) freeze motion, making it ideal for action shots. Slower speeds (e.g., 1/30s) create motion blur, which can add an artistic effect. The camera

will adjust the aperture for a balanced exposure.

4. **Manual Mode (M)**:
   - In Manual Mode, you have complete control over both aperture and shutter speed. This is best for situations where you want full creative control, such as long-exposure shots or studio photography.
5. **Program Mode (P)**:
   - Program Mode is semi-automatic. The camera sets the aperture and shutter speed for a balanced exposure, but you can still adjust other settings like ISO, white balance, and focus mode.

Control Dials: How to Adjust Shutter Speed, Aperture, and ISO

The Sony A7R V has control dials on the front and back. Let's go over how to use them for key settings:

1. **Front Control Dial**:
   - By default, this dial usually adjusts the aperture. For example, if you're in Aperture Priority Mode (A), turning the front dial changes the f-stop (aperture value), affecting how much light enters the camera and the depth of field.
2. **Rear Control Dial**:
   - This dial is typically set to adjust the shutter speed. In Shutter Priority Mode (S), turning the rear dial will let you control the shutter speed, influencing how motion is captured.
3. **ISO Settings**:
   - You can adjust ISO sensitivity by assigning it to a custom button or using the menu. ISO affects the camera's sensitivity to light; higher

ISO (e.g., 1600) brightens images but may add noise, while lower ISO (e.g., 100) keeps images clean but requires more light.

Custom Buttons (C1, C2, C3, etc.): Assigning Functions for Quick Access

The custom buttons (C1, C2, C3, etc.) are located around the camera body, allowing you to quickly access specific settings. Here's how to set them up and some ideas on what you might want to assign:

1. **How to Set Up Custom Buttons**:
   - Open the **Menu**, go to **Setup**, and look for **Custom Key Settings**. Here, you can assign different functions to each custom button.
2. **Common Assignments**:
   - **C1 for ISO**: Quick access to adjust ISO without going into the menu.
   - **C2 for White Balance**: Helpful for quickly adapting to different lighting.
   - **C3 for Focus Area**: Ideal for switching between focus areas, such as Wide or Flexible Spot, depending on the scene.

Customizing these buttons can save you a lot of time, especially in fast-paced shooting environments where you need to adjust settings quickly.

AF-On Button: Focusing Options and Customization

The AF-On button, located near the viewfinder, is used to activate autofocus independently of the shutter button. This is helpful because it allows you to focus and recompose your shot without worrying about losing focus when you press the shutter.

1. **Using the AF-On Button**:
   - To use, press and hold the AF-On button to focus on your subject. Release it once you're satisfied with the focus, then press the shutter button to take the shot. This setup is often called "back-button focus."
2. **Customizing AF-On for Different Focus Modes**:
   - The A7R V allows you to customize how the AF-On button behaves. For example, you can assign different autofocus modes, like **Continuous AF** for moving subjects or **Single AF** for still subjects, to get the best results for different scenarios.

Other Important Buttons and Functions

1. **AEL (Auto Exposure Lock) Button**:
   - The AEL button, usually located near the AF-On button, locks the exposure. This means the camera keeps the same brightness level even if the lighting changes. This is useful for scenes with uneven lighting, like backlit portraits.
2. **Multi-Selector (Joystick)**:
   - The joystick helps you move the focus point around the screen quickly. Simply press and push the joystick in any direction to move your focus area.
3. **Focus Mode Switch** (if available on the lens):
   - Some Sony lenses have a switch for choosing between AF (autofocus) and MF (manual focus). AF is helpful for fast shooting, while MF lets you focus manually by turning the focus ring on the lens.
4. **Playback Button**:
   - Located on the back of the camera, the Playback button lets you review photos and

videos you've just taken. You can zoom in to
check focus or browse through your shots to
decide which ones to keep.

5. **Delete Button**:
    o   When you're in playback mode, press the
        Delete button to remove unwanted photos or
        videos. The camera will ask for confirmation
        before deleting.

Master the Rule of Thirds, then Break It

The rule of thirds is a great starting point for balanced compositions. Position your subject along the lines or intersections of a 3x3 grid. Once you're comfortable, don't hesitate to break the rule for creative compositions, especially if it adds drama or a unique perspective to your shot.

Chapter Five

Mastering Autofocus

AI-Based Autofocus System: How It Works

The Sony A7R V features an advanced autofocus (AF) system powered by AI (Artificial Intelligence). This system can recognize and track subjects like humans, animals, and even vehicles. Using the camera's AI-based processing, the autofocus can detect faces, eyes, and moving objects with incredible precision.

- **Face and Eye Detection**: The camera automatically detects faces and focuses on eyes, which is especially useful for portrait photography. You can even choose whether it should focus on the left or right eye.
- **Animal and Bird Tracking**: This mode is designed to track animals in motion. It's helpful for wildlife photographers who need to keep moving subjects sharp.
- **Vehicle Tracking**: For motorsports or fast-moving vehicles, the camera can detect and track cars and other moving objects, making it versatile for various types of photography.

This AI-based autofocus helps you capture clear, sharp photos, even in challenging situations where the subject is moving quickly.

Tracking Subjects: Humans, Animals, and Vehicles

Sony has made it easy to customize the AF tracking for different subjects. Here's how you can adjust your settings depending on what you're shooting:

1. **For Portraits (Humans)**:
    o **Set Focus Mode to Continuous AF (AF-C)**: This mode continuously adjusts focus as the subject moves, ensuring their face or eyes stay sharp.
    o **Activate Face/Eye Priority in AF**: This option detects and focuses on the subject's eyes. To set this, go to the AF settings in the menu and turn on Face/Eye Priority in AF.
    o **Select Left or Right Eye**: You can choose which eye the camera should prioritize. This can be helpful for creative compositions where you want one eye in sharper focus.
2. **For Wildlife (Animals and Birds)**:
    o **Set Focus Mode to AF-C**: Continuous AF keeps the camera focused on fast-moving animals.
    o **Choose Animal/Bird Recognition**: In the AF settings, select Animal or Bird as your subject. The camera will track the animal's face or body, and for some animals, it even detects eyes.
3. **For Action (Vehicles and Sports)**:
    o **Use Zone or Wide Focus Area**: These settings allow the camera to focus on a larger area, which is helpful when tracking fast-moving subjects.
    o **Enable Vehicle Tracking**: Go to the AF settings and choose the option for vehicle tracking. This is useful for capturing sharp images of cars, bikes, or other fast vehicles.

Customizing Autofocus Modes

The Sony A7R V offers different AF modes to suit different scenes. Here's a breakdown of each mode and when to use it:

1. **Single-Shot AF (AF-S)**:
   - o   Best for still subjects. The camera focuses once when you press the shutter halfway and holds that focus until you take the shot.
2. **Continuous AF (AF-C)**:
   - o   Ideal for moving subjects. The camera continuously adjusts focus as the subject moves. This is commonly used for action, wildlife, or sports photography.
3. **DMF (Direct Manual Focus)**:
   - o   This mode lets you use autofocus to get close to focus and then fine-tune with the manual focus ring on the lens. It's helpful for precise focusing in challenging conditions.
4. **Manual Focus (MF)**:
   - o   You control focus entirely. Use this mode when autofocus might struggle, like in low-light or low-contrast situations, or for creative control over focus points.

Best AF Settings for Different Scenarios

Let's go over some common scenarios and the best autofocus settings to use for each:

1. **Portrait Photography**:
   - o   **Focus Mode**: AF-C (Continuous AF)
   - o   **Focus Area**: Flexible Spot or Wide (to cover the subject's face)
   - o   **Face/Eye Priority**: On (choose left or right eye if needed)

   This setup ensures the camera locks onto the subject's face or eyes and follows them as they move slightly.

2. **Sports and Action Photography**:
   - o   **Focus Mode**: AF-C

- o **Focus Area**: Zone or Wide
- o **Subject Recognition**: Choose Vehicle Tracking if needed

This setup helps keep a fast-moving subject sharp, using a larger focus area so the camera can track motion more effectively.

3. **Wildlife Photography**:
   - o **Focus Mode**: AF-C
   - o **Focus Area**: Wide (to capture unpredictable movement)
   - o **Subject Recognition**: Animal or Bird (depending on your subject)

For wildlife, the camera will recognize and focus on animals' faces or eyes, helping you get sharp shots even if the animal is moving quickly.

4. **Landscape Photography**:
   - o **Focus Mode**: AF-S (Single-Shot AF)
   - o **Focus Area**: Flexible Spot or Wide

Since landscapes are stationary, Single-Shot AF works well. Using Flexible Spot or Wide ensures the scene is in sharp focus without needing to track movement.

Tips for Getting the Most from Your Autofocus

Here are some practical tips to get the best results from the A7R V's autofocus:

1. **Use Back-Button Focus (AF-On)**: By assigning focus to the AF-On button, you separate focus from the shutter. This is useful if you want to lock focus on a specific spot and recompose your shot.

2. **Customize AF Speed and Sensitivity**: In the menu, you can adjust how quickly the AF tracks moving subjects and how sensitive it is to changes in movement. For fast action, a higher sensitivity helps; for slower subjects, a lower sensitivity can prevent jumping focus.
3. **Check Your Focus Points in Playback**: After taking a shot, use playback to review where the camera focused. This helps ensure that the AF is working as intended and lets you adjust settings if needed.
4. **Use Flexible Spot for Precision**: If you need precise focus on a specific part of your subject (like an eye), use Flexible Spot. Move the focus point using the joystick to place it exactly where you want.

Capture Emotion and Movement

Photos that capture raw emotion or motion bring an image to life. Use a slower shutter speed to capture movement (such as waves or city traffic) for a sense of dynamism, or focus on expressions to tell a deeper story that resonates emotionally.

Chapter Six

Shooting Modes and Advanced Settings

Using the Intelligent Auto Mode

Intelligent Auto Mode is a fully automatic mode where the camera makes all the decisions for you. It's represented by a green icon on the Mode Dial and is perfect for beginners or quick shots where you don't want to worry about settings.

- **How It Works**: In this mode, the camera analyzes the scene in front of it and adjusts the settings accordingly. It chooses the best combination of aperture, shutter speed, and ISO for you. This includes detecting faces, adjusting focus, and even recognizing specific types of scenes like portraits, landscapes, or close-ups.
- **When to Use It**: Intelligent Auto is ideal for quick snapshots, casual photography, or times when you're focusing more on the moment than on fine-tuning settings.

Scene Selection Modes: When and How to Use Them

The A7R V also includes specific **Scene Modes** tailored for different types of scenes. These modes adjust settings to optimize for certain environments, making it easier to capture the intended look.

1. **Portrait Mode**: Softens the background to emphasize the subject. Ideal for capturing people and focusing on the face.

2. **Landscape Mode**: Boosts colors and sharpens details, making it great for scenic shots with a wide depth of field.
3. **Sports Action Mode**: Uses a fast shutter speed to freeze motion, ideal for capturing moving subjects like people in motion, animals, or sports.
4. **Macro Mode**: Optimized for close-up shots, this mode works well for capturing small details, such as flowers, insects, or other tiny subjects.
5. **Night Scene**: Adjusts for low-light conditions, often slowing the shutter speed and increasing ISO to capture more light. Best used with a tripod to avoid blur.
6. **Sunset Mode**: Enhances warm tones to make sunsets look vibrant and dramatic.

- **How to Select Scene Modes**: Rotate the Mode Dial to "SCN," then use the menu or the touchscreen to select the specific scene you want.
- **When to Use Them**: Scene modes are helpful when you know the environment you're shooting in but don't want to manually adjust settings.

Understanding Exposure: Manual Mode vs. Auto Mode

Exposure determines how bright or dark your image will be, and it's affected by three main settings: **Aperture, Shutter Speed**, and **ISO**. Let's break down how these work in different modes:

1. **Auto Mode**:
   - In Auto Mode, the camera automatically balances aperture, shutter speed, and ISO to ensure a well-lit photo. It's quick and convenient but offers limited creative control.
2. **Manual Mode (M)**:

- o   Manual Mode gives you complete control over exposure. You can adjust each setting (aperture, shutter speed, and ISO) individually.
- o   **Aperture**: Controls the depth of field. Lower f-stops (e.g., f/2.8) create a blurred background, while higher f-stops (e.g., f/16) keep more of the scene in focus.
- o   **Shutter Speed**: Controls how long the sensor is exposed to light. Faster speeds (e.g., 1/1000s) freeze action, while slower speeds (e.g., 1/30s) can create motion blur.
- o   **ISO**: Controls the camera's sensitivity to light. Higher ISO settings brighten the image but can introduce grain or noise.

Tip: For those new to Manual Mode, start by setting one variable (such as aperture) and letting the camera's exposure meter guide you to balance the other two.

Metering Modes: Spot, Center-Weighted, and Multi

Metering is how the camera reads light in the scene to determine the right exposure. The A7R V has three main metering modes:

1. **Multi (Multi-Segment) Metering**:
   - o   This mode measures light across the entire frame, dividing it into multiple zones. It then balances exposure based on the overall scene.
   - o   **When to Use**: Ideal for most general situations, as it provides a balanced exposure that works well for landscapes, portraits, and scenes with even lighting.
2. **Center-Weighted Metering**:
   - o   Focuses on the center of the frame while considering some of the surrounding areas.

It's helpful when the subject is in the middle and you want it exposed properly without distractions from the edges.

- o **When to Use**: Use this mode for portraits or when your subject is in the center and the background doesn't need as much focus.

3. **Spot Metering**:
   - o This mode measures a small spot in the frame, typically at the center or wherever your focus point is. It only considers this specific area for exposure.
   - o **When to Use**: Great for high-contrast scenes where you want to expose specifically for one part of the image (e.g., a person's face in backlighting).

How to Adjust Metering Modes:

- Go to **Menu > Exposure > Metering Mode** and select the desired option. Try different modes to see how each affects the look of your photos.

Advanced Exposure Modes: Aperture Priority and Shutter Priority

For those who want more control than Auto but aren't ready to go fully manual, **Aperture Priority (A)** and **Shutter Priority (S)** are semi-manual modes.

1. **Aperture Priority (A)**:
   - o In this mode, you set the aperture (f-stop), and the camera chooses the shutter speed for a balanced exposure. This mode is perfect for controlling depth of field.
   - o **Example Use**: For portraits with a blurred background, use a lower f-stop (e.g., f/2.8) in

Aperture Priority. For landscapes where you want everything in focus, use a higher f-stop (e.g., f/11).

2. **Shutter Priority (S)**:
   - Here, you set the shutter speed, and the camera adjusts the aperture. This mode is useful for capturing or freezing motion.
   - **Example Use**: To freeze action in sports or wildlife photography, choose a fast shutter speed (e.g., 1/1000s). For creative blur, such as light trails or smooth water, use a slower speed (e.g., 1/15s or slower) and consider using a tripod.

ISO Settings: Auto vs. Manual

ISO is an important part of exposure and can be set to Auto or Manual depending on your needs.

1. **Auto ISO**:
   - In Auto ISO, the camera adjusts the ISO automatically based on the lighting conditions. You can set a maximum ISO value to avoid excessive grain.
   - **When to Use**: Useful in fast-changing light conditions, such as moving between indoors and outdoors.
2. **Manual ISO**:
   - You control the ISO setting. Lower values (e.g., ISO 100) are ideal for bright conditions, while higher values (e.g., ISO 1600 or 3200) are better for low light.
   - **When to Use**: Manual ISO is best when you need consistent exposure or want to minimize noise in your images.

How to Set ISO:

- You can set ISO through the menu or by assigning it to a custom button for easy access.

Chapter Seven

Mastering Exposure and ISO

Exposure is a combination of three main settings: **Aperture**, **Shutter Speed**, and **ISO**. Together, these settings determine how much light reaches the camera sensor, affecting the brightness and quality of your image. Understanding how to adjust each one gives you control over the look and feel of your photos, whether you want a bright scene, a dramatic shadow, or minimal noise.

How to Adjust Exposure Settings

The Sony A7R V provides several ways to adjust exposure based on your shooting mode:

1. **Aperture**: Controls the size of the lens opening.
   - A lower f-stop (e.g., f/2.8) allows more light, creating a bright image with a shallow depth of field (blurred background).
   - A higher f-stop (e.g., f/16) restricts light, creating a darker image with a deeper depth of field (more in focus).
   - **Adjusting Aperture**: Use Aperture Priority Mode (A) or Manual Mode (M) to control this setting. Turn the front control dial to select your desired f-stop.
2. **Shutter Speed**: Determines how long the sensor is exposed to light.
   - Faster speeds (e.g., 1/1000s) freeze motion, allowing less light in.
   - Slower speeds (e.g., 1/30s) create motion blur and allow more light.
   - **Adjusting Shutter Speed**: Use Shutter Priority Mode (S) or Manual Mode (M) to

adjust this. Turn the rear control dial to set the shutter speed.

3. **ISO**: Sets the camera sensor's sensitivity to light.
    o   A lower ISO (e.g., ISO 100) results in less sensitivity, which keeps images clean and sharp.
    o   A higher ISO (e.g., ISO 1600) makes the sensor more sensitive to light but can introduce noise (graininess).
    o   **Adjusting ISO**: Set this through the menu or by assigning it to a custom button for easy access.

Understanding ISO Sensitivity

ISO affects how your camera handles light. Here's a closer look at how to make the most of ISO settings in different lighting conditions:

1. **Low ISO (e.g., ISO 100–200)**:
    o   Ideal for bright conditions or well-lit environments, such as outdoor photography on a sunny day.
    o   Produces clean, noise-free images, preserving detail and color.
2. **Medium ISO (e.g., ISO 400–800)**:
    o   Suitable for indoor or cloudy outdoor settings where there's less light.
    o   Produces slightly more noise but keeps a good balance between brightness and quality.
3. **High ISO (e.g., ISO 1600+)**:
    o   Used for low-light conditions, such as night photography or indoor scenes with minimal lighting.
    o   Increases image brightness but introduces more noise. The A7R V handles high ISO well, but it's best to use only when necessary.

Tip: To keep noise under control, set an ISO limit in the camera settings (e.g., ISO 3200), so the camera doesn't automatically go beyond that limit in Auto ISO mode.

Best Practices for Low-Light Photography

The A7R V performs well in low-light settings, but here are some tips to get the best results:

1. **Use a Wide Aperture (Low f-stop)**:
   - A wider aperture (e.g., f/2.8) allows more light, which is ideal for low-light conditions. If you're shooting a portrait, this also creates a pleasing blur in the background.
2. **Increase Shutter Speed Carefully**:
   - A slower shutter speed lets in more light but can cause motion blur if handheld. For night shots, consider using a tripod to keep the camera steady at slower shutter speeds.
3. **Increase ISO as Needed**:
   - Raise the ISO to brighten the image if you can't use a wider aperture or slower shutter speed. Be mindful of noise, especially at very high ISO values.
4. **Turn on Image Stabilization**:
   - The Sony A7R V has in-body image stabilization (IBIS) that helps reduce blur when shooting handheld in low light. This feature allows you to use slower shutter speeds without introducing motion blur.

ISO Auto vs. Manual: When to Use Each

Both Auto and Manual ISO have their benefits, depending on your shooting style and the situation.

1. **Auto ISO**:
   - In Auto ISO, the camera adjusts ISO based on the lighting conditions, keeping exposure balanced. You can set a maximum ISO limit to prevent excessive noise.
   - **When to Use**: Auto ISO is ideal for dynamic scenes where lighting changes quickly, like events or moving between indoor and outdoor locations.
2. **Manual ISO**:
   - In Manual ISO, you control the sensitivity. It's best when you want consistent image quality, or if you're in a controlled lighting environment (like a studio).
   - **When to Use**: Manual ISO is preferred for low-light photography where noise control is critical or for scenes where you want full creative control over the exposure.

Setting ISO Limits for Auto ISO:

- To keep your images noise-free, go to **Menu > ISO Settings > Max Auto ISO** and set an upper limit, such as ISO 1600 or ISO 3200. This helps the camera maintain image quality in auto mode.

Using Exposure Compensation

Exposure compensation lets you quickly adjust brightness without changing other settings. It's helpful in tricky lighting situations where the camera might not capture the scene as bright or dark as you'd like.

1. **How to Use Exposure Compensation**:
   - Turn the **Exposure Compensation Dial** (marked with + and -) on the top right of the camera. Adjust to a positive value (+) to

brighten the image or a negative value (-) to darken it.

2. **When to Use Exposure Compensation**:
   - **Backlit Subjects**: Increase exposure to keep the subject from appearing too dark.
   - **Snowy or Bright Scenes**: Decrease exposure to prevent over-brightening.
   - **Creative Effects**: Play with overexposure or underexposure to add drama or mood to your photos.

Additional Tips for Controlling Exposure and ISO

1. **Enable Highlight Warning**:
   - This setting shows a warning (highlight "blinkies") on the LCD screen for overexposed areas. It helps you avoid blown-out highlights where detail is lost.
2. **Use Exposure Bracketing**:
   - Exposure bracketing takes multiple shots at different exposures. It's useful in high-contrast scenes, allowing you to choose the best exposure or merge them later for HDR images.
3. **Check Your Histogram**:
   - The histogram displays the distribution of light in your image. A balanced histogram (not overly skewed to the left or right) usually means a well-exposed photo. Use it to check exposure, especially in tricky lighting.
4. **Shoot in RAW for Greater Flexibility**:
   - RAW files retain more detail in shadows and highlights, making it easier to adjust exposure and reduce noise in post-processing.

Change your perspective to uncover hidden angles. Shoot from above, below, or at eye level to add diversity and interest. Unusual angles can make even familiar subjects look fresh and captivating, helping you discover unexpected beauty.

Chapter Eight

White Balance and Color Management

White balance and color management are crucial for making your photos look natural and true-to-life. Different types of light can add color tints to your images. For example, indoor lighting can create a warm (yellow) tint, while shade outdoors might make photos look cool (blue). White balance helps correct these tints to make colors look natural. Let's explore the white balance settings on the Sony A7R V and how to use color profiles for creative control.

Adjusting White Balance for Different Lighting Conditions

The Sony A7R V offers several white balance presets that you can use to adjust color quickly. Each preset is tailored for a specific type of lighting.

1. **Auto White Balance (AWB)**:
    - This mode automatically adjusts the white balance based on the lighting conditions. It's a great choice for general photography, especially when lighting changes quickly.
    - **When to Use**: Auto White Balance works well in mixed lighting or when you're moving between different lighting sources, like indoors to outdoors.
2. **Daylight**:
    - Optimized for shooting outdoors in natural sunlight. This setting provides a neutral color balance for bright, sunny conditions.
    - **When to Use**: Perfect for sunny days when you want natural color tones.
3. **Shade**:

- o Adds warmth to counteract the cool, blue tones often found in shaded areas.
  - o **When to Use**: Ideal for outdoor shots taken in the shade or on cloudy days when colors can appear too cool.
4. **Cloudy**:
   - o Adds a slight warmth to neutralize the coolness of overcast skies, similar to Shade but less intense.
   - o **When to Use**: Great for overcast days or slightly shaded scenes.
5. **Tungsten**:
   - o Corrects for the warm, yellow-orange tint of indoor lighting. This mode cools down the colors, making indoor shots appear more natural.
   - o **When to Use**: Use when shooting indoors under standard light bulbs.
6. **Fluorescent**:
   - o Corrects the greenish tint of fluorescent lighting, giving a more neutral color tone.
   - o **When to Use**: Ideal for indoor shots under fluorescent lights, common in offices and commercial spaces.
7. **Flash**:
   - o Adds a touch of warmth to balance the cool light from the camera's flash.
   - o **When to Use**: Useful when using an on-camera flash, especially for indoor portraits.

How to Select White Balance Presets:

- Go to **Menu > White Balance** and choose your desired preset. Experiment with each setting to see how it affects the color in different lighting conditions.

Using Custom White Balance for Precision

Custom White Balance is a powerful feature on the Sony A7R V that allows you to manually set the color temperature based on the specific lighting conditions. This option is especially useful in challenging lighting environments where presets might not deliver accurate colors.

1. **Setting Custom White Balance**:
    o In the **White Balance menu,** select **Custom Setup**.
    o Point the camera at a white or neutral-colored surface (like a white sheet of paper) under the current lighting.
    o Press the shutter to take a reading. The camera will measure the color temperature and adjust white balance based on the light in that environment.
2. **Manual Color Temperature Setting**:
    o You can also adjust the color temperature manually by selecting a specific **Kelvin (K) value**. Lower values (e.g., 3000K) make the image cooler, while higher values (e.g., 7000K) warm it up.
    o **Example**: For warm indoor lighting, set a Kelvin value around 3000-4000K; for daylight, use 5000-6500K.

When to Use Custom White Balance:

- Custom White Balance is ideal for unique lighting conditions where none of the presets match, such as mixed light sources or unusual lighting colors.

Picture Profiles: S-Log3, HLG, and More for Video and Photo

The Sony A7R V offers Picture Profiles, which are advanced color settings designed for both photography and videography. These profiles can help you achieve specific looks or prepare footage for color grading in post-processing. Here are some of the most common profiles:

1. **Standard Picture Profile**:
    - Delivers balanced contrast, saturation, and sharpness. It's the default setting and suitable for general use.
    - **When to Use**: Ideal for everyday photography and videos when you don't need heavy color grading.
2. **S-Log3**:
    - S-Log3 is a flat color profile that captures a wider range of tones and details in shadows and highlights. It's designed for color grading in post-production, giving you flexibility in editing.
    - **When to Use**: Great for professional videographers or photographers who want maximum control over color and exposure in post-processing.
3. **HLG (Hybrid Log-Gamma)**:
    - HLG is designed for high dynamic range (HDR) content, capturing more detail in bright and dark areas. This profile produces vivid images without the need for extensive post-processing.
    - **When to Use**: Ideal for HDR-ready displays or when shooting in challenging lighting with high contrast.
4. **Cine Profiles (e.g., Cine1, Cine2)**:

- o These profiles deliver a cinematic look with lower contrast, useful for a more filmic appearance. They are also easier to edit compared to standard profiles.
- o **When to Use**: Perfect for narrative-style videos or photo projects where you want a cinematic feel.

How to Set Picture Profiles:

- Go to **Menu > Picture Profile** and choose from available options. Each profile can be further customized for sharpness, contrast, and color settings.

Tips for Effective Color Management

1. **Shoot in RAW for Flexibility**:
   - o RAW files retain all the color data, making it easier to adjust white balance and color in post-processing without losing quality.
2. **Use a Gray Card for Accurate White Balance**:
   - o A gray card helps set a precise white balance in custom mode by giving the camera a neutral reference point.
3. **Match Profiles Across Devices**:
   - o If you're using multiple cameras or shooting in different lighting environments, keep your color settings consistent by using the same white balance and picture profiles across devices.
4. **Experiment with Color for Creative Effects**:
   - o White balance and color profiles aren't only for correcting colors; they can also create artistic effects. For example, a cooler white balance (around 4000K) can create a moody, blue-toned scene, while warmer settings (around 6000K) add a golden glow.

Chapter Nine

In-Body Image Stabilization (IBIS)

In-body image stabilization (IBIS) is a powerful feature in the Sony A7R V. This stabilization system compensates for small movements or shakes, keeping your images and videos sharp. The A7R V's IBIS uses 5-axis stabilization, which means it corrects for movements along five different axes. Let's explore how IBIS works, when to use it, and how to get the best results.

How IBIS Works

The A7R V's IBIS system has a sensor inside the camera that detects tiny movements and shakes. When it senses movement, it adjusts the position of the camera sensor to counteract the shake. This makes a huge difference in handheld shooting by reducing blur, particularly at slower shutter speeds.

- **5-Axis Stabilization**: The Sony A7R V compensates for five types of movement:
    1. **Pitch (up and down)**
    2. **Yaw (left and right)**
    3. **Roll (rotation)**
    4. **Horizontal shift**
    5. **Vertical shift**

This advanced stabilization allows you to capture sharp images, even at slower shutter speeds, which is useful for low-light photography and video.

When to Use Image Stabilization

While IBIS can be helpful in many situations, it's especially useful in specific scenarios:

1. **Low-Light Photography**:
   o   In low-light conditions, you often need a slower shutter speed to let in more light. IBIS compensates for small shakes when using slower shutter speeds, so you can capture sharp images even without a tripod.
2. **Handheld Video Recording**:
   o   IBIS provides smoother footage for handheld video, reducing jittery movements. This stabilization is especially helpful for video in places where a tripod or gimbal isn't practical.
3. **Telephoto and Macro Lenses**:
   o   When using longer focal lengths, even the smallest movement can create blur. IBIS minimizes shake, making it easier to get sharp photos with telephoto lenses or in macro photography.
4. **Shooting in Windy or Unstable Conditions**:
   o   IBIS can help reduce blur when shooting outdoors in windy conditions or from a moving vehicle, where small vibrations are common.

Best Settings for Handheld Shots and Low Light

The Sony A7R V lets you adjust stabilization settings, so you can optimize IBIS depending on the type of shot you're taking. Here's how to get the best results:

1. **Enable SteadyShot**:

- o **SteadyShot** is Sony's name for their stabilization system. To turn it on, go to **Menu > Stabilization > SteadyShot** and select **On**.
- o **When to Turn Off**: If you're using a tripod, it's generally best to turn off SteadyShot, as the stabilization system might try to compensate for non-existent movement, which can result in subtle blur.

2. **Adjust SteadyShot Settings for Specific Lenses**:
   - o For some lenses, especially those without their own built-in stabilization, you can manually set the focal length in the SteadyShot settings. Go to **Menu > Stabilization > SteadyShot Settings** and select the focal length you're using (e.g., 50mm, 85mm).
   - o **Why This Matters**: Accurate focal length helps the camera apply the right amount of stabilization, ensuring sharper results.

3. **Use a Moderate Shutter Speed**:
   - o While IBIS helps with slower shutter speeds, it's best to keep the shutter speed at a moderate level for maximum sharpness. As a general rule, try using a shutter speed that matches or is faster than your focal length (e.g., 1/50s for a 50mm lens).

4. **Pair with a Fast Aperture and Low ISO**:
   - o When shooting handheld in low light, use a wide aperture (low f-stop) to let in more light, allowing for a lower ISO setting. This minimizes noise and enhances sharpness, making IBIS even more effective.

Using IBIS for Video

In video mode, IBIS can greatly improve the stability of your footage. Here's how to optimize stabilization for video shooting:

1. **Enable Active SteadyShot for Video**:
   - The A7R V has an **Active SteadyShot** mode, which provides additional stabilization for video recording. This mode applies slight cropping to enhance stability.
   - **When to Use Active SteadyShot**: This setting is best for handheld video or when walking while recording, as it significantly reduces jitter and helps create smoother motion.
2. **Combine with a Gimbal for Maximum Stability**:
   - While IBIS does a great job on its own, combining it with a gimbal can produce even smoother, cinematic video footage, especially for action shots or complex movements.
3. **Avoid Excessive Panning or Fast Movements**:
   - IBIS works best for steady shots. If you need to pan quickly or capture high-speed movement, consider turning off IBIS to avoid any lag in stabilization.

Practical Tips for Effective Image Stabilization

1. **Use a Firm Grip**:
   - Holding the camera steadily makes IBIS even more effective. Keep your elbows close to your body and use a two-handed grip for more control.
2. **Shoot in Bursts**:
   - If you're using a slower shutter speed, try taking a burst of shots. The A7R V's IBIS

helps, but shooting in bursts increases the chances of getting a sharp shot as it compensates for slight hand movements.

3. **Set a Low ISO to Minimize Noise**:
   - Since IBIS allows you to use slower shutter speeds, you can often avoid raising the ISO too high in low-light conditions. Lower ISO settings produce cleaner images with less noise, which is especially important in night photography.

4. **Practice Slow and Controlled Movements**:
   - For video, move slowly and deliberately. While IBIS helps reduce shake, smooth and steady motion complements the stabilization, resulting in professional-looking video.

5. **Check Your Image Sharpness**:
   - After taking a shot, zoom in during playback to ensure sharpness. This helps confirm that IBIS effectively compensated for shake, especially in low-light shots.

Limitations of IBIS

While IBIS is powerful, it's not a complete substitute for a tripod in extremely low-light or very long-exposure photography. Here's when you might still want to use a tripod:

- **Long Exposures (Over 1 Second)**: For night photography or long exposures, IBIS may not be enough to counteract all movement. Use a tripod to ensure maximum sharpness.
- **Macro Photography with Very Small Subjects**: While IBIS helps in macro shots, even slight movement can affect tiny subjects. For extremely close-ups, a tripod provides the best stability.

Incorporate foreground, midground, and background elements to add dimension and context to your shots. Layering can bring a scene to life by creating a sense of place and time, inviting viewers to feel like they're stepping into the moment with you.

Chapter Ten

Advanced Video Settings

The Sony A7R V is packed with professional-grade video features that allow you to capture stunning footage. With options for 8K and 4K resolution, various frame rates, and customizable color profiles, you can tailor your video settings for everything from cinematic films to high-speed action.

Shooting in 8K: How to Set Up and Maximize Quality

The A7R V's 8K recording capability captures extremely high-resolution video with stunning detail. Here's how to set it up and make the most of it:

1. **Setting Up 8K Video**:
    - Go to **Menu > Movie Settings > Record Settings** and select **8K**.
    - 8K resolution provides four times the detail of 4K, which is great for projects that require cropping in post-production or displaying on large screens.
2. **Considerations for 8K**:
    - **Storage**: 8K files are large and require a fast, high-capacity memory card. Use **CFexpress Type A** cards for faster data transfer and smooth recording.
    - **Battery Life**: 8K recording consumes more battery power. Consider bringing extra batteries or using a power source like a USB-C power bank.
    - **Heat Management**: 8K video can generate heat, especially during extended recording. Keep an eye on the camera's temperature

warning and avoid prolonged recording in hot environments.

3. **When to Use 8K**:
   - 8K is ideal for high-end projects where maximum detail is required, or when you plan to crop the footage in editing. It's also beneficial for landscape videography, where capturing fine details adds to the visual impact.

4K Recording at 60fps: What You Need to Know

The Sony A7R V can also record in 4K at up to 60 frames per second (fps), providing smooth, high-quality footage suitable for most professional projects.

1. **Setting Up 4K 60fps**:
   - Go to **Menu > Movie Settings > Record Settings** and select **4K 60p**.
   - 4K 60fps allows you to capture smooth motion, making it great for action, sports, or scenes where you may want to use slow-motion effects.
2. **When to Use 4K 60fps**:
   - **Action Shots**: Capturing high-speed movement with 60fps results in smooth video playback and enables high-quality slow motion.
   - **B-Roll and Cinematic Effects**: Recording at 60fps lets you slow down footage for cinematic effects in post-production.
3. **Benefits of 4K Over 8K**:
   - 4K video takes up less storage than 8K, making it more manageable for longer projects. It's also easier to process on most computers, which helps in faster editing.

Frame Rates and Bit Depth: Understanding the Options

The Sony A7R V offers a range of frame rates and bit depths, giving you control over the quality and feel of your video.

1. **Common Frame Rates**:
   - **24fps**: The standard frame rate for a cinematic look.
   - **30fps**: Often used for smooth video with slightly less motion blur.
   - **60fps**: Ideal for smooth playback and slow motion when slowed down in editing.
   - **120fps** (4K): Available for extreme slow motion in lower resolutions; ideal for creative effects.
2. **Choosing the Right Bit Depth**:
   - **8-Bit vs. 10-Bit**: The Sony A7R V supports both 8-bit and 10-bit color depth. 10-bit records more color information, providing richer colors and smoother gradients, which is useful for color grading.
   - **4:2:2 vs. 4:2:0 Color Sampling**: 4:2:2 offers more color information, making it ideal for professional video where color grading is important.

Setting Bit Depth and Frame Rate:

- Go to **Menu > Movie Settings > Record Settings** to adjust frame rate and bit depth. Choose 10-bit 4:2:2 for maximum color quality when you plan to edit and grade the footage.

Using Picture Profiles for Video: S-Log and HLG

Sony's Picture Profiles allow you to adjust the look of your footage, with options specifically for video, such as **S-Log** and **HLG (Hybrid Log-Gamma)**.

1. **S-Log3**:
   - **What It Does**: S-Log3 is a flat color profile that captures a wide dynamic range, retaining detail in shadows and highlights.
   - **When to Use**: Ideal for professional projects where you plan to do extensive color grading in post-production. S-Log3 provides a lot of flexibility but requires editing to bring out colors and contrast.
   - **Setting Up**: Go to **Menu > Picture Profile** and select **PP8** (usually S-Log3). Adjust settings like Gamma and Color Mode to customize further.
2. **HLG (Hybrid Log-Gamma)**:
   - **What It Does**: HLG is a high dynamic range (HDR) profile that captures bright and dark areas well without as much need for editing. It's designed to look good right out of the camera.
   - **When to Use**: HLG is useful when you want HDR video without heavy post-processing, especially for direct playback on HDR-ready screens.
   - **Setting Up**: Go to **Menu > Picture Profile** and select **PP10** (usually HLG). This mode can be viewed in HDR on compatible monitors, enhancing the dynamic range.
3. **Cine Profiles (e.g., Cine1, Cine2)**:
   - **What They Do**: Cine profiles offer a more cinematic look with lower contrast and softer

highlights, making them ideal for narrative videos or film-style footage.

- o **When to Use**: Perfect for projects that need a filmic look without heavy color grading.
- o **Setting Up**: Access Cine profiles through **Picture Profile**, typically PP1 to PP4.

External Recording Options and Accessories

For those looking to push the Sony A7R V's video capabilities further, using an external recorder and accessories can enhance quality and flexibility.

1. **External Recorders**:
   - o **Why Use an External Recorder**: External recorders like the Atomos Ninja V allow you to record in higher-quality formats (e.g., ProRes) and avoid compression limits.
   - o **Setting Up**: Connect the external recorder through the **HDMI port** on the A7R V. Go to **Menu > HDMI Settings** and adjust settings as needed for output quality.
2. **External Microphones**:
   - o **Why Use an External Microphone**: Built-in camera mics can pick up unwanted sounds. Using a shotgun or lavalier microphone improves audio quality.
   - o **Setting Up**: Connect the microphone to the **Mic Input** on the camera, and adjust audio levels in the **Menu > Audio Recording Settings**.
3. **ND Filters for Exposure Control**:
   - o ND (Neutral Density) filters reduce the amount of light entering the lens, allowing for a slower shutter speed or wider aperture in bright conditions, which is great for achieving a cinematic look in daylight.

4. **Using a Gimbal for Stabilization**:
    o   While the A7R V has excellent in-body stabilization, using a gimbal can further enhance video stability, especially during movement or tracking shots. Popular options include DJI and Zhiyun gimbals, which help smooth out handheld footage.

Tips for Professional Video Results

1. **Set a Custom White Balance**:
    o   Setting a custom white balance for each scene ensures accurate colors and reduces the need for color correction in editing.
2. **Use a High-Quality Memory Card**:
    o   High-bitrate 4K and 8K videos require fast write speeds. Use **V90 SD cards** or **CFexpress Type A** cards for smooth recording without dropped frames.
3. **Optimize Settings for Lighting Conditions**:
    o   Adjust Picture Profiles or white balance based on lighting, and consider using a reflector or external lighting for controlled shoots.
4. **Experiment with Frame Rates for Creative Effects**:
    o   Higher frame rates (60fps, 120fps) allow for slow motion, while 24fps adds a classic cinematic feel.

Chapter Eleven

Wireless and Connectivity Features

How to Set Up Wi-Fi, Bluetooth, and NFC

Let's start by setting up the wireless connections, which allow you to connect your camera with other devices and transfer files wirelessly.

1. **Wi-Fi Setup**:
   - Go to **Menu > Network > Wi-Fi Settings** and turn on Wi-Fi.
   - **Wi-Fi Direct**: If you want to connect directly to a smartphone or computer, select **Wi-Fi Direct**. This establishes a direct connection without needing a router.
   - **Wi-Fi Network**: To connect to a local Wi-Fi network, choose **Access Point Settings** and select your network from the list. Enter the password if required.
2. **Bluetooth Setup**:
   - Bluetooth provides a low-energy connection for maintaining a stable link between your camera and smartphone.
   - Go to **Menu > Network > Bluetooth Settings** and turn on Bluetooth.
   - Open the **Imaging Edge Mobile** app on your smartphone, and pair it with the camera by following the prompts. Once connected, Bluetooth allows you to geotag images and maintain a connection for file transfer.
3. **NFC (Near Field Communication)**:
   - NFC lets you quickly pair your camera with compatible devices by simply bringing them close to each other.

- To use NFC, enable it in **Menu > Network > NFC Settings**.
- Tap your NFC-enabled smartphone to the camera's NFC logo to establish a connection automatically, which opens the Imaging Edge Mobile app for remote control or file transfer.

Transferring Files to Smartphones and Computers

Once your connections are set up, you can transfer files wirelessly, making it easy to share photos on social media or save them to your computer.

1. **Transfer to Smartphone**:
   - Open the **Imaging Edge Mobile** app on your phone, and choose **Send to Smartphone** from the camera's playback menu.
   - You can select individual photos or batches to transfer. The app allows you to save photos in full resolution or a smaller size for faster sharing.
2. **Transfer to Computer**:
   - With Wi-Fi, you can send images directly to a computer if it's on the same network.
   - Go to **Menu > Network > Send to Computer**. You'll need to install **Imaging Edge Desktop** on your computer and set up a pairing between the devices. This option allows for automatic backup as you shoot.
3. **Auto Transfer**:
   - If you'd like images to transfer automatically after each shot, enable **Auto Transfer** in the Network settings. This is especially useful for studio photography or tethered shooting where you want each photo to appear on your computer right away.

Remote Control and Tethered Shooting Options

The Sony A7R V offers remote control capabilities, allowing you to operate the camera from a smartphone or computer, which is helpful for group photos, self-portraits, or shots that require camera stability.

1. **Remote Control with Smartphone**:
   - Open the **Imaging Edge Mobile** app and choose **Remote Control**.
   - You can adjust settings like aperture, shutter speed, ISO, and focus remotely. The live view is displayed on your smartphone screen, letting you frame and capture shots without touching the camera.
2. **Tethered Shooting with Imaging Edge Desktop**:
   - Tethered shooting is when your camera is connected to a computer, allowing you to view and control shots in real-time.
   - Install **Imaging Edge Desktop** on your computer. Connect the camera using a USB-C cable, then open the software and select **Remote (Tethered Shooting)**.
   - In this mode, you can control all settings, preview images on a larger screen, and transfer files directly to your computer. Tethered shooting is popular in studio photography, where precise control and immediate feedback are needed.
3. **Remote Control with External Devices**:
   - Besides a smartphone or computer, you can also use **wireless remote controls** compatible with Sony cameras. These are useful for long-exposure shots, astrophotography, or time-lapse photography, where you want to avoid camera shake.

Additional Connectivity Features

The Sony A7R V includes several other connectivity options that can enhance your workflow:

1. **FTP (File Transfer Protocol)**:
   - The A7R V supports FTP, allowing you to transfer files directly to a server over Wi-Fi. This feature is valuable for professionals who need to send images immediately after capture, such as event photographers or journalists.
   - To set up FTP, go to **Menu > Network > FTP Transfer Settings**. You'll need to enter the server details, including the IP address, port, and login information.
2. **HDMI Output**:
   - The A7R V's **HDMI port** lets you connect the camera to an external monitor or recorder. This is useful for video recording, as you can monitor footage on a larger screen or record in higher quality.
   - **Setup**: Connect the HDMI cable to an external monitor or recorder, and go to **Menu > HDMI Settings** to adjust resolution and output settings.
3. **USB-C Connectivity**:
   - The **USB-C port** on the A7R V can be used for tethered shooting, charging, or connecting to other devices for file transfer.
   - **Tethered Charging**: The camera can be powered through USB-C while shooting, which is useful for extended shooting sessions.
4. **Geotagging with Bluetooth**:
   - When connected to a smartphone via Bluetooth, the A7R V can receive GPS data

from the phone, allowing you to geotag images. This feature is helpful for travel photography, as it records the exact location of each shot.

Tips for Using Wireless and Connectivity Features

1. **Maintain Battery Life**:
   - Wireless features can consume battery power quickly. If you're shooting for long periods, consider turning off Wi-Fi and Bluetooth when not in use or use a USB-C power bank to extend battery life.
2. **Optimize Image Transfer Settings**:
   - For faster transfers, reduce the file size when sending images to your smartphone. Full-resolution files take longer to send, especially over Wi-Fi.
3. **Check Network Compatibility**:
   - Wi-Fi settings vary depending on networks. Make sure your camera's network settings are compatible with the network type (e.g., 2.4GHz or 5GHz).
4. **Update Imaging Edge Apps Regularly**:
   - Sony frequently updates the Imaging Edge Mobile and Desktop apps to improve performance and add new features. Keeping these apps up-to-date ensures smooth connectivity.

Chase the Golden Hour
The warm, soft light during sunrise and sunset brings out
colors and textures that create a magical quality in your
images. Experiment with this natural light to add warmth and
depth to your photos, and take advantage of the long
shadows to add dimension.

Chapter Twelve

Memory and Data Management

Choosing the Right Memory Card: SD and CFexpress Compatibility

The A7R V has dual memory card slots, compatible with **SD cards** and **CFexpress Type A cards**. Understanding the differences between these options will help you choose the right cards for your shooting needs.

1. **CFexpress Type A Cards**:
   - **Speed**: CFexpress Type A cards offer very high read and write speeds, making them ideal for 8K video, high-bitrate 4K, and high-speed continuous shooting. These cards ensure the camera can save data quickly, reducing lag.
   - **Capacity**: CFexpress cards come in large storage capacities, which is helpful when shooting in high-resolution formats.
   - **Cost**: CFexpress Type A cards are more expensive than SD cards but are worth the investment if you frequently shoot 8K video or high-bitrate footage.
2. **SD Cards (UHS-II Recommended)**:
   - **Speed**: SD UHS-II cards are fast and suitable for most photography and 4K video recording. Look for cards with high speed ratings (e.g., V60 or V90) to ensure smooth recording and fast write speeds.
   - **Capacity**: SD cards are more affordable than CFexpress cards, making them a practical choice for general photography or lower-bitrate video.

o   **Best Use**: If you mainly shoot still photos or standard 4K video, SD cards are a reliable and cost-effective choice.

Setting Card Preferences:

- Go to **Menu > Media Settings > Recording Media Settings** to set preferences. You can choose which slot to use as the primary recording location or set one slot for photos and the other for videos.

Formatting and Managing Cards in Camera

Formatting memory cards is important for keeping them optimized and preventing file corruption. Regular formatting helps ensure the cards work efficiently and are compatible with the camera.

1. **How to Format a Card**:
   o   Insert the memory card into the camera, go to **Menu > Setup > Format**, and select the card you want to format. Formatting erases all data on the card, so be sure to back up any files you need before formatting.
2. **Switching Between Slots**:
   o   With dual card slots, you can set the camera to **Auto Switch** between Slot 1 and Slot 2. This feature is helpful for long shoots, as the camera will automatically switch to the second card when the first card is full.
3. **Assigning Functions to Each Slot**:
   o   You can assign different media types to each slot. For example, set Slot 1 for RAW images and Slot 2 for JPEGs, or use one slot for videos and the other for photos. Go to **Menu > Media Settings > Recording Mode** to configure these settings.

For professional photographers and videographers, keeping your data secure is crucial. Here are some strategies to help you back up and protect your work.

1. **Dual Slot Recording**:
   - The Sony A7R V allows **simultaneous recording** to both memory card slots. This setup creates an automatic backup, ensuring that all images or videos are saved to two cards. In **Menu > Recording Mode**, choose **Simultaneous Recording** to enable this feature.
   - **When to Use**: This is highly recommended for events, weddings, or critical shoots where you cannot afford to lose data.
2. **Offloading Files After Each Shoot**:
   - After a shoot, offload files to an external hard drive or computer. Create folders to organize files by date, client, or project for easy access.
   - Consider using an external SSD for faster transfer speeds, especially with large files from 8K video or high-resolution images.
3. **Cloud Backup**:
   - For additional security, consider backing up files to a cloud storage service like Google Drive, Dropbox, or a dedicated photography backup service. This ensures you have a secure, offsite copy of your files in case of hardware failure or loss.
   - **Tip**: Use cloud backup software that automatically syncs folders on your computer to save time.
4. **Using Backup Software**:
   - Backup software can automate the process of copying files from your memory card to an

external drive and a cloud service simultaneously. Look for options like Adobe Lightroom, which also offers photo management, or dedicated backup solutions like Carbon Copy Cloner (Mac) or Acronis (Windows).

Optimizing Storage and File Management

Managing data effectively saves storage space and improves workflow efficiency. Here are a few tips to optimize storage:

1. **Use JPEG and RAW Only When Needed**:
    - If you don't need RAW files for every photo, consider shooting in JPEG-only mode for general shots and RAW for important, high-detail images. This will save space on your memory cards and simplify post-processing.
2. **Delete Unwanted Files Regularly**:
    - After each shoot, review your images and delete any you won't use. This frees up space on your memory cards and storage devices, keeping your library organized.
3. **Organize Files with Naming Conventions**:
    - Use a consistent naming convention for folders and files. For example, structure folders by date (YYYYMMDD) or by project/client name, so you can quickly locate files when needed.
    - In-camera, you can set file names to start with custom characters (e.g., "EVT" for events or "PJT" for personal projects) in **Menu > File Settings**.
4. **Consider External RAID Storage for Large Projects**:
    - If you handle large volumes of files, an external RAID storage system offers high

capacity and redundancy. RAID systems
duplicate data across multiple drives,
protecting against data loss while providing
quick access.

Setting Up and Managing In-Camera File Types

Understanding the difference between file formats and
knowing when to use each can make data management easier:

1. **RAW**:
   - RAW files contain all the image data captured
     by the sensor, providing maximum flexibility
     in editing but taking up more space. RAW is
     ideal for projects that require fine-tuning in
     post-production.
2. **JPEG**:
   - JPEG files are compressed, smaller, and
     suitable for quick sharing or when you don't
     need extensive editing. JPEG files take up less
     space and are useful for online sharing or
     client previews.
3. **HEIF**:
   - HEIF (High-Efficiency Image File) format
     offers high-quality images at smaller file sizes,
     suitable for storage-saving without
     compromising quality. Note that HEIF may
     not be compatible with all devices or
     software, so use it when you know
     compatibility is not an issue.

How to Select File Types:

- Go to **Menu > Quality/Image Size** and choose
  your preferred format (RAW, JPEG, or HEIF). You
  can also select the image quality and compression
  level for JPEGs to balance quality and storage needs.

Practical Tips for Effective Data Management

1. **Use High-Capacity Cards for Video and High-Resolution Images**:
   o If you're shooting 8K or large RAW files, high-capacity cards (128GB or more) prevent interruptions from changing cards frequently.
2. **Label and Track Cards**:
   o Label each memory card with a number or color code to keep track of full or empty cards. This makes it easier to rotate cards without accidentally overwriting or losing data.
3. **Carry a Card Case**:
   o Keep memory cards organized and protected with a dedicated card case. This helps prevent cards from getting lost, damaged, or mixed up.
4. **Regularly Clean Up and Archive Older Projects**:
   o Periodically review and move completed projects to an external drive or cloud storage to free up space on your primary storage device.

Chapter Thirteen

Essential Accessories for Sony A7R V

Recommended Lenses for Every Type of Photography

Different lenses allow you to capture a variety of scenes with unique perspectives. Here are some popular lens types and suggestions for the Sony A7R V:

1. **Standard Zoom Lenses**:
   - **Sony FE 24-70mm f/2.8 GM II**: This lens is a favorite for general-purpose shooting, providing a versatile range from wide to short telephoto. With a constant f/2.8 aperture, it performs well in low-light situations and delivers a beautiful background blur.
   - **When to Use**: Great for portraits, landscapes, and everyday shooting. Its zoom range makes it adaptable for various scenarios.
2. **Prime Lenses**:
   - **Sony FE 50mm f/1.8**: This lens is compact and lightweight, offering excellent image quality with a wide aperture for low light and shallow depth of field.
   - **Sony FE 85mm f/1.4 GM**: This prime lens is perfect for portraits, creating stunning background separation and delivering sharp images with creamy bokeh.
   - **When to Use**: Prime lenses are ideal for low-light photography, portraits, and when you want high image quality with minimal distortion.
3. **Wide-Angle Lenses**:
   - **Sony FE 16-35mm f/2.8 GM**: A versatile wide-angle zoom, this lens is great for

capturing landscapes, architecture, and interiors. The wide-angle range allows for creative compositions and dramatic perspectives.

- **When to Use**: Best for landscapes, architectural shots, and situations where you need a broad field of view.

4. **Telephoto Lenses**:
   - **Sony FE 70-200mm f/2.8 GM OSS**: This telephoto zoom lens is essential for capturing distant subjects with precision. It features image stabilization (OSS) for sharp handheld shots.
   - **When to Use**: Ideal for wildlife, sports, and portrait photography, where you need to zoom in on subjects from a distance.

5. **Macro Lenses**:
   - **Sony FE 90mm f/2.8 Macro G OSS**: A dedicated macro lens that allows you to get close-up shots with incredible detail. It's perfect for photographing small subjects, like flowers or insects.
   - **When to Use**: Best for macro photography, product shots, and situations where you want extreme close-ups with sharp detail.

External Microphones, Monitors, and Flash Units

External accessories can greatly improve the quality of your videos and photos, especially in professional shooting environments.

1. **External Microphones**:
   - **Sony ECM-B1M Shotgun Microphone**: This compact shotgun microphone provides clear audio for video recording and attaches directly to the camera's Multi Interface Shoe.

- o **Rode VideoMic Pro+**: Another popular choice for vloggers and filmmakers, this shotgun mic offers high-quality sound and is compatible with the A7R V's mic input.
  - o **When to Use**: Ideal for recording interviews, vlogs, and videos where clear audio is essential.
2. **External Monitors**:
  - o **Atomos Ninja V**: This external monitor allows for 4K recording and provides a larger screen to view footage, making it easier to check composition, focus, and exposure.
  - o **When to Use**: Helpful for video recording, especially in complex setups where you need precise control over focus and exposure.
3. **Flash Units**:
  - o **Sony HVL-F60RM**: A powerful on-camera flash unit with wireless control capabilities. It allows for flexible lighting setups and supports high-speed sync.
  - o **Godox V1**: A third-party flash with a round head design for softer, more natural lighting. It's affordable and versatile for indoor and outdoor photography.
  - o **When to Use**: Ideal for portrait, event, and low-light photography where you need additional light for balanced exposure.

Using Gimbals and Tripods for Stabilization

To capture steady shots and smoother videos, consider using stabilizers like gimbals and tripods.

1. **Gimbals**:
  - o **DJI Ronin-SC**: A lightweight gimbal for mirrorless cameras, providing smooth

stabilization for handheld video. It's easy to set up and great for on-the-go videography.

- o **Zhiyun Crane 2S**: Known for its sturdy build and versatility, this gimbal offers smooth stabilization and compatibility with various lenses and accessories.
- o **When to Use**: Perfect for handheld video, especially in dynamic shots where you're moving around. Gimbals reduce shake and create smooth, cinematic footage.

2. **Tripods**:
   - o **Manfrotto Befree Advanced**: A compact and lightweight travel tripod, ideal for stability in both photography and videography.
   - o **Gitzo Series 2 Traveler**: Known for its durability and lightness, this tripod is a solid choice for professional and travel photographers.
   - o **When to Use**: Great for long exposures, landscape photography, low-light shots, and any situation where stability is critical.

Best Camera Bags, Batteries, and Chargers

Keeping your camera safe and ready for shooting is easier with the right bags, batteries, and charging solutions.

1. **Camera Bags**:
   - o **Peak Design Everyday Backpack**: A versatile bag with customizable dividers, making it easy to organize your camera gear. It's comfortable for long shoots and travel.
   - o **Lowepro ProTactic 450 AW II**: This rugged bag offers excellent protection and plenty of compartments for organizing lenses, accessories, and your camera body.

o   **When to Use**: Ideal for photographers on the move, allowing you to carry all essential gear safely and comfortably.

2. **Batteries**:
    o   **Sony NP-FZ100 Battery**: The official battery for the A7R V, known for its longevity. Having extra batteries ensures you won't run out of power during extended shoots.
    o   **Wasabi Power NP-FZ100**: A reliable third-party option compatible with the A7R V, offering similar performance at a lower cost.
    o   **When to Use**: Essential for long shooting sessions, especially when shooting video or in cold environments where batteries drain faster.
3. **Battery Chargers**:
    o   **Sony BC-QZ1 Battery Charger**: A fast charger for NP-FZ100 batteries, allowing you to quickly charge multiple batteries.
    o   **Dual USB-C Charger**: Consider a dual charger to charge two batteries simultaneously, which is handy for travel or long shoots.
    o   **When to Use**: Great for ensuring all batteries are ready before a long shoot or trip.

Additional Useful Accessories

1. **ND Filters**:
    o   **Tiffen Variable ND Filter**: This adjustable filter allows you to control the amount of light entering the lens, ideal for achieving a cinematic look in bright light.
    o   **When to Use**: ND filters are useful in bright conditions when you want a slower shutter speed or wider aperture without overexposing.

2. **Remote Shutter Release**:
   - o **Sony RMT-P1BT**: A wireless remote that lets you trigger the shutter without touching the camera, helping to reduce camera shake in long exposures.
   - o **When to Use**: Useful for night photography, time-lapse, or any setup where you don't want to touch the camera directly.
3. **Lens Cleaning Kit**:
   - o **Giottos Rocket Air Blaster and Zeiss Lens Cleaning Kit**: A must-have for keeping lenses clean. This kit includes a blower, microfiber cloth, and lens cleaning solution.
   - o **When to Use**: Regular cleaning keeps your lenses free from dust and smudges, maintaining image clarity.
4. **Memory Card Case**:
   - o **Pelican Memory Card Case**: This waterproof and shockproof case keeps memory cards safe and organized. It's essential for professional shoots where multiple cards are in use.
   - o **When to Use**: Perfect for organizing and protecting memory cards, especially during travel or outdoor shoots.

Chapter Fourteen

Practical Shooting Scenarios

Portrait Photography: Best Settings and Techniques

Portraits benefit from a sharp focus on the subject's eyes, a flattering background blur, and accurate skin tones. Here's how to set up the A7R V for portrait success:

1. **Use a Prime Lens with a Wide Aperture**:
   - Lenses like the **Sony FE 85mm f/1.4 GM** or **Sony FE 50mm f/1.8** provide a shallow depth of field, creating a beautiful background blur (bokeh) that isolates your subject.
2. **Focus Settings**:
   - **Focus Mode**: Set to **AF-C (Continuous AF)**, which keeps the subject in focus as they move.
   - **Focus Area**: Use **Flexible Spot** or **Wide** with **Face/Eye AF** enabled, ensuring the camera locks onto the subject's eyes.
3. **Exposure Settings**:
   - **Aperture**: Choose a wide aperture (e.g., f/1.8 to f/2.8) to create background blur and draw attention to the subject.
   - **Shutter Speed**: Keep it around 1/125s or faster to prevent motion blur.
   - **ISO**: Use the lowest ISO possible for a clean image, adjusting as needed for lighting conditions.
4. **White Balance**:
   - Use **Auto White Balance** or set a custom white balance for consistent skin tones. You can also set the camera to **Daylight** or **Shade** to warm up tones outdoors.

5. **Composition Tips**:
    o   Frame the subject's face to leave a bit of space
        around them, and try using the rule of thirds
        for a balanced composition.

Landscape Photography: Maximizing Detail and Depth

Landscapes benefit from a sharp image across the scene,
vibrant colors, and a high depth of field. Here's how to set up
the A7R V for stunning landscapes:

1. **Lens Choice**:
    o   Wide-angle lenses like the **Sony FE 16-35mm
        f/2.8 GM** or the **Sony FE 24-70mm f/2.8
        GM** capture expansive views and bring out
        detail in the foreground and background.
2. **Focus Settings**:
    o   **Focus Mode**: Set to **AF-S (Single-Shot AF)**
        for stationary scenes.
    o   **Focus Area**: Use **Flexible Spot** or **Wide**
        focus area, and focus on a point about one-
        third into the scene to achieve a large depth of
        field.
3. **Exposure Settings**:
    o   **Aperture**: Use a smaller aperture (e.g., f/8 to
        f/16) to keep the entire scene in focus.
    o   **Shutter Speed**: Use a tripod if you're
        shooting at slower speeds to avoid camera
        shake. If handheld, keep it at 1/60s or faster.
    o   **ISO**: Set to ISO 100 or 200 to reduce noise
        and capture clear details.
4. **White Balance**:
    o   Set to **Daylight** or **Cloudy** for natural color
        balance. You can also adjust it manually for
        warm or cool tones based on the time of day.
5. **Additional Tips**:

o   Use **HDR (High Dynamic Range)** or
    Exposure Bracketing to capture a wider
    dynamic range, especially when shooting
    scenes with bright skies and dark shadows.

Sports and Wildlife: High-Speed Shooting and Autofocus Tips

Capturing fast-moving subjects requires quick autofocus and
high shutter speeds. Here's how to set up your camera for
sports and wildlife photography:

1. **Lens Choice**:
    o   Telephoto lenses like the **Sony FE 70-
        200mm f/2.8 GM OSS** or **Sony FE 100-
        400mm f/4.5-5.6 GM OSS** allow you to
        capture distant subjects and provide excellent
        sharpness.
2. **Focus Settings**:
    o   **Focus Mode**: Set to **AF-C (Continuous AF)**
        to track moving subjects.
    o   **Focus Area**: Use **Zone** or **Wide** focus area to
        help the camera lock onto fast-moving
        subjects.
    o   **Animal Eye AF**: For wildlife, enable **Animal
        Eye AF** to lock onto animals' eyes.
3. **Exposure Settings**:
    o   **Shutter Speed**: Set to 1/1000s or faster to
        freeze action. For very fast movements,
        consider 1/2000s or higher.
    o   **Aperture**: Use a wide aperture (e.g., f/2.8 to
        f/5.6) to create background separation and
        isolate the subject.
    o   **ISO**: Increase ISO as needed to maintain a
        fast shutter speed, especially in low light.
4. **Drive Mode**:

o   Set to **Continuous Shooting (High)** for burst mode, allowing you to capture multiple frames per second. This increases the chance of capturing the perfect moment.

5. **Additional Tips**:
    o   Use **Back-Button Focus** (assign focus to the AF-ON button) to separate focusing from the shutter release. This technique allows for continuous focus without needing to press the shutter halfway.

Low-Light and Night Photography: Getting Crisp Shots in the Dark

Low-light photography requires specific settings to balance exposure, prevent noise, and reduce motion blur. Here's how to get sharp, bright images in low light:

1. **Lens Choice**:
    o   Fast lenses with wide apertures, such as the **Sony FE 24mm f/1.4 GM** or **Sony FE 50mm f/1.8**, are excellent for low light because they allow more light to reach the sensor.
2. **Focus Settings**:
    o   **Focus Mode**: Use **AF-S (Single-Shot AF)** if your subject is stationary. In extremely low light, consider switching to **Manual Focus** for precision.
    o   **Focus Area**: Use **Flexible Spot** and focus on a bright part of the scene or a spot with contrast to help the camera lock onto the subject.
3. **Exposure Settings**:
    o   **Aperture**: Set to the widest available aperture (e.g., f/1.8 to f/2.8) to let in maximum light.

- o **Shutter Speed**: Use a slower shutter speed (e.g., 1/30s or slower) if using a tripod, but increase the shutter speed (e.g., 1/60s) for handheld shots to prevent blur.
  - o **ISO**: Increase ISO as needed to achieve a balanced exposure. With the A7R V's good noise control, you can often go up to ISO 3200 or 6400 without significant noise.

4. **White Balance**:
   - o Set to **Auto White Balance** or **Tungsten** for indoor scenes to balance warm lighting. For outdoor night shots, consider **Daylight** or **Custom** settings.
5. **Stabilization and Tripod**:
   - o Use **In-Body Image Stabilization (IBIS)** for handheld shots to reduce shake. For long-exposure shots, a tripod is essential for keeping the camera steady.
6. **Additional Tips**:
   - o Enable **Long Exposure Noise Reduction** in the menu to reduce noise in long-exposure shots. Use **Exposure Compensation** if the scene is too bright or dark.

Additional Scenario: Street Photography

Street photography requires quick reactions and flexibility. Here's how to optimize your camera for capturing candid moments in urban settings:

1. **Lens Choice**:
   - o A compact, fast prime lens like the **Sony FE 35mm f/1.8** or **Sony FE 50mm f/1.8** is ideal for street photography, as it's lightweight and provides a natural perspective.
2. **Focus Settings**:

- o **Focus Mode**: Set to **AF-C (Continuous AF)** if capturing moving subjects, or **AF-S** for stationary subjects.
- o **Focus Area**: Use **Flexible Spot** for precise focusing, or **Zone** if you're capturing wider scenes.

3. **Exposure Settings**:
   - o **Aperture**: Use a mid-range aperture (e.g., f/4 to f/5.6) to keep both subject and background sharp while allowing enough light.
   - o **Shutter Speed**: Set to 1/125s or faster to prevent motion blur. If needed, increase ISO to maintain speed.

4. **Drive Mode**:
   - o Use **Single Shooting** for precise moments or **Continuous Shooting** if capturing fast action on the street.

5. **Additional Tips**:
   - o Enable **Silent Shutter Mode** to shoot discreetly, especially in quiet environments. This helps you capture candid moments without drawing attention.

Chapter Fifteen

Maintenance and Troubleshooting

Taking care of your camera is essential to ensure it remains reliable and delivers high-quality images. This chapter covers maintenance routines, firmware updates, and solutions to common problems you might encounter with the Sony A7R V.

Cleaning and Maintaining Your Camera

Regular cleaning and proper storage protect your camera from dust, dirt, and accidental damage. Here are the key areas to keep clean and how to safely maintain your camera.

1. **Cleaning the Lens**:
   - Use a **blower** to remove dust and loose particles from the lens surface.
   - Gently wipe the lens with a **microfiber cloth** or lens tissue and lens-cleaning solution if needed. Wipe in a circular motion to avoid streaks.
   - **Tip**: Always use a **UV filter** on your lens to protect it from scratches and dust.
2. **Cleaning the Sensor**:
   - The Sony A7R V has a **Sensor Cleaning Mode** that automatically vibrates the sensor to remove dust. To activate this, go to **Menu > Setup > Cleaning Mode**.
   - For persistent dust spots, use a **sensor cleaning kit** specifically designed for mirrorless cameras. Avoid touching the sensor directly and follow the cleaning instructions carefully.

- o **Tip**: When changing lenses, always point the camera downward to reduce dust entering the sensor area.

3. **Cleaning the Camera Body**:
   - o Wipe the camera body with a soft, lint-free cloth. Avoid using liquid cleaners, as they may damage the exterior.
   - o Clean the viewfinder and LCD screen with a microfiber cloth. For stubborn smudges, slightly dampen the cloth with water.

4. **Battery Maintenance**:
   - o Remove the battery when the camera is not in use for extended periods, and store it in a cool, dry place.
   - o Charge batteries regularly, even if they're not in use, to prolong their lifespan. Avoid completely draining the battery, as it can reduce its capacity over time.

5. **Storage**:
   - o Store your camera in a dry, dust-free area. A **camera bag** or **protective case** with desiccant packs helps reduce moisture and prevents dust buildup.
   - o Avoid exposing the camera to extreme temperatures. Prolonged exposure to heat or cold can affect battery life and camera performance.

Firmware Updates: How and Why to Keep Your Camera Updated

Sony periodically releases firmware updates for the A7R V to improve performance, add features, and fix bugs. Updating your firmware ensures your camera functions optimally.

1. **Checking for Firmware Updates**:

o   Visit Sony's support website to check if a firmware update is available for the A7R V. Download the latest firmware if there's an update.

2. **Updating Firmware**:
   o   Connect the camera to your computer with a **USB-C cable**.
   o   Follow the instructions provided on Sony's support page. Make sure your battery is fully charged before beginning the update.
   o   **Tip**: Do not turn off the camera or disconnect it during the update, as this can cause issues with the firmware installation.

3. **Benefits of Firmware Updates**:
   o   Firmware updates often include performance improvements, new features, and compatibility fixes. Regular updates help ensure your camera operates smoothly.

Troubleshooting Common Problems

Even with regular maintenance, you may occasionally run into issues. Here's a guide to troubleshooting some of the most common problems:

1. **Autofocus Issues**:
   o   **Problem**: The camera struggles to lock focus, especially in low light or with fast-moving subjects.
   o   **Solution**: Ensure you're using the correct **Focus Mode** (AF-S for still subjects, AF-C for moving subjects). Enable **Focus Area** settings like **Flexible Spot** or **Wide** to help the camera focus on specific areas.
   o   **Additional Tip**: Clean the lens and sensor, as dust or smudges can affect focus accuracy.

2. **Overheating During Extended Video Recording**:

o **Problem**: The camera shuts down due to overheating during long video sessions, especially in 8K or high-bitrate 4K.

o **Solution**: Use a **cooling setup** or allow breaks between recordings to prevent overheating. For extended video, record in lower resolutions or use **external power** to avoid battery heating.

o **Additional Tip**: Avoid direct sunlight and use the camera in shaded or cooler environments.

3. **Slow Performance or Lag**:

o **Problem**: The camera responds slowly, especially in continuous shooting or 4K video recording.

o **Solution**: Use a **high-speed memory card** (CFexpress Type A or UHS-II SD card) to ensure smooth performance. Regularly format memory cards to keep them optimized.

o **Additional Tip**: Check for firmware updates, as updates can improve performance and resolve software issues.

4. **Battery Drains Quickly**:

o **Problem**: The battery drains faster than expected, especially when using wireless features.

o **Solution**: Turn off **Wi-Fi, Bluetooth**, and **NFC** when not in use. Lower the **screen brightness** and **use the viewfinder** instead of the LCD for longer battery life.

o **Additional Tip**: Consider carrying extra batteries or a USB-C power bank for extended shoots.

5. **Image Quality Issues**:

o **Problem**: Images appear blurry, noisy, or have inconsistent color.

- o **Solution**: Ensure the **ISO** is set appropriately for lighting conditions to avoid excessive noise. Adjust **White Balance** settings for accurate colors. Clean the lens and sensor to avoid dust and smudges affecting clarity.
  - o **Additional Tip**: Use a tripod or image stabilization for sharpness, especially in low-light situations or long exposures.

6. **Camera Freezes or Unresponsive**:
   - o **Problem**: The camera freezes or becomes unresponsive to inputs.
   - o **Solution**: Turn off the camera, remove the battery, wait for a few seconds, and then reinsert it. Restart the camera. If the issue persists, perform a **factory reset** (found in the Setup menu) or check for a firmware update.
   - o **Additional Tip**: If using third-party accessories, remove them to ensure they're not causing conflicts.

Preventative Maintenance Tips

To reduce the chances of problems arising, follow these tips for ongoing care:

1. **Update Firmware Regularly**:
   - o Keep your camera updated to benefit from performance enhancements and bug fixes.
2. **Format Memory Cards in Camera**:
   - o Format memory cards regularly to prevent data corruption. Always format in-camera rather than using a computer to ensure compatibility.
3. **Check Your Gear Before Shoots**:
   - o Before heading out, ensure all batteries are charged, lenses are clean, and memory cards

are formatted and empty. This simple routine can save time and avoid surprises on location.

4. **Use Weather Sealing**:
    - The A7R V is weather-sealed, but additional protection like a **camera rain cover** can keep your gear safe in challenging weather conditions, preventing moisture damage.
5. **Handle Lenses Carefully**:
    - When changing lenses, avoid exposing the camera's sensor to dust by keeping the camera body facing downwards. Always use lens caps and protective cases when storing lenses.

Common Problems and Step-by-Step Solutions for the Sony A7R V

1. Autofocus Not Locking on Subject

Problem: The autofocus struggles to lock onto a subject, especially in low-light conditions or with fast-moving objects.

Solution:

1. **Select Appropriate Focus Mode:**
   - Go to **Menu > AF/MF** and ensure **AF-C (Continuous AF)** is selected for moving subjects or **AF-S (Single-Shot AF)** for still subjects.
2. **Enable Face/Eye AF:**
   - Activate **Face/Eye AF** in **Menu > Face/Eye AF Settings** for people, or **Animal Eye AF** for pets and wildlife.
3. **Adjust Focus Area:**
   - Choose **Flexible Spot** for precise control, or **Zone** if you're capturing a larger area. This can be found under **Focus Area** in the AF menu.
4. **Use Manual Focus in Extreme Low-Light:**
   - If autofocus struggles in very dark environments, switch to **Manual Focus** using the **AF/MF selector** on the camera body and use focus peaking to assist.

2. Camera Overheating During Long Video Recording

Problem: The camera overheats and shuts down during extended 8K or 4K recording sessions.

Solution:

1. **Reduce Recording Quality**:
   - Try switching from 8K to 4K or reduce the bitrate in **Menu > Record Settings** to reduce processing demands.
2. **Take Breaks During Recording**:
   - Allow breaks between shots and let the camera cool down if it feels warm. Move the camera to a cooler area or shade if shooting outdoors.
3. **Use External Power**:
   - Use an external **USB-C power source** instead of relying on the internal battery, which generates more heat during extended use.
4. **Enable Auto Power Off Temp**:
   - Go to **Menu > Power Settings > Auto Power OFF Temp** and set it to **High**. This allows the camera to continue operating at higher temperatures, though caution is recommended.

3. Images Are Blurry or Out of Focus

Problem: Images appear blurry or have poor focus, even in good lighting.

Solution:

1. **Check Shutter Speed**:
   - o Ensure your shutter speed is fast enough for handheld shots. Use at least **1/60s for stationary subjects** or faster for moving subjects.
2. **Enable In-Body Image Stabilization (IBIS)**:
   - o Go to **Menu > Stabilization > SteadyShot** and enable IBIS to reduce camera shake for handheld shots.
3. **Clean the Lens and Sensor**:
   - o Dust or smudges on the lens or sensor can cause blurred images. Use a blower to clean the sensor, and gently clean the lens with a microfiber cloth.
4. **Use Manual Focus for Precision**:
   - o For challenging shots, switch to **Manual Focus** using the **AF/MF selector**. Use **Focus Magnifier** in the menu to zoom in and check focus accuracy.

4. Memory Card Errors or Slow Write Speed

Problem: Memory card errors or slow performance when recording high-bitrate video or shooting in continuous mode.

Solution:

1. **Use High-Speed Cards**:
   - o Use **CFexpress Type A or UHS-II SD cards** with high speed ratings (V90 or higher for SD cards) to ensure smooth recording and fast data transfer.
2. **Format the Card In-Camera**:
   - o Regularly format memory cards in the camera to prevent file corruption. Go to **Menu > Setup > Format** and select the card to format.

3. **Switch to Slot 2 If Necessary**:
   - If the primary card is slow or corrupted, try switching to Slot 2. Go to **Menu > Media Settings > Recording Mode** and set Slot 2 as the primary.

5. Battery Drains Quickly

Problem: The battery drains faster than expected, especially during extended sessions.

Solution:

1. **Disable Wi-Fi, Bluetooth, and NFC**:
   - Go to **Menu > Network Settings** and turn off Wi-Fi, Bluetooth, and NFC when not in use to conserve power.
2. **Lower Screen Brightness**:
   - Set the screen brightness to a lower setting in **Menu > Display > Monitor Brightness**.
3. **Use Airplane Mode**:
   - Enable **Airplane Mode** in **Network Settings** to disable all wireless connections, which significantly reduces battery consumption.
4. **Use External Power**:
   - For extended sessions, use an external power bank or AC adapter connected to the **USB-C port** for continuous power.

6. Camera Freezes or Becomes Unresponsive

Problem: The camera becomes unresponsive or freezes while shooting.

Solution:

1. **Restart the Camera**:
   - o Turn off the camera, remove the battery, wait for a few seconds, and then reinsert the battery before turning it back on.
2. **Reset Settings**:
   - o If the issue persists, reset the camera settings by going to **Menu > Setup > Reset Settings**.
3. **Update Firmware**:
   - o Check for firmware updates on Sony's official website and update to the latest version to fix any potential software bugs.

7. Inconsistent Color or White Balance in Images

Problem: Images have inconsistent colors, or white balance appears off across multiple shots.

Solution:

1. **Set a Custom White Balance**:
   - o If lighting conditions are challenging, set a custom white balance by going to **Menu > White Balance > Custom Setup**. Take a reading from a neutral gray or white card.
2. **Choose the Correct White Balance Preset**:
   - o Choose the most appropriate white balance preset (e.g., Daylight, Cloudy, Tungsten) based on the lighting situation.
3. **Use AWB Lock for Consistency**:
   - o If using **Auto White Balance (AWB)**, enable AWB Lock in **White Balance Settings** to keep white balance consistent throughout a series of shots.

8. Slow Autofocus in Low-Light Conditions

Problem: Autofocus performance slows down significantly in dim lighting.

Solution:

1. **Enable Focus Assist**:
   - Go to **Menu > Focus Assist Settings** and enable **Focus Peaking** to help identify in-focus areas in low light.
2. **Use Center Focus**:
   - Set **Focus Area** to **Center** or **Flexible Spot** to increase focusing accuracy in low light.
3. **Increase Exposure for Improved AF**:
   - Increase ISO or use a wider aperture to allow more light into the lens, which can improve autofocus performance.
4. **Consider Using Manual Focus**:
   - If autofocus continues to struggle, switch to **Manual Focus** for better control, especially for still subjects.

9. Images Have Excessive Noise in Low Light

Problem: Low-light photos have excessive noise, even at moderate ISO settings.

Solution:

1. **Lower the ISO if Possible**:
   - Use the lowest ISO possible for the lighting conditions to reduce noise. Aim for ISO 800 or lower in most low-light scenarios.
2. **Use a Wider Aperture**:

o   Open up the aperture to let in more light, which helps you maintain lower ISO settings.

3. **Enable Long Exposure Noise Reduction**:
    o   In **Menu > Noise Reduction > Long Exposure NR**, enable this option to reduce noise in long exposures.

4. **Post-Processing**:
    o   For additional noise reduction, use software like Adobe Lightroom or Capture One Pro, which offer effective noise-reduction tools.

10. The Camera Won't Power On

Problem: The camera doesn't turn on, even when pressing the power button.

Solution:

1. **Check Battery Charge**:
    o   Ensure the battery is fully charged. Insert a freshly charged battery if the current one might be drained.

2. **Inspect Battery Compartment and Terminals**:
    o   Ensure the battery compartment is clean and that battery terminals are free of dust or debris that might disrupt the connection.

3. **Reset the Camera**:
    o   Remove the battery, wait for a minute, then reinsert it and try turning on the camera again.

4. **Try an Alternate Power Source**:
    o   If possible, connect a USB-C power bank or AC adapter to see if the camera turns on with an external power source.

www.ingramcontent.com/pod-product-compliance
Lightning Source LLC
Chambersburg PA
CBHW071926120726
48001CB00005B/1889